W9-AVM-240

Slim Goodbody's Life Skills 101

CAN WE BE FRIENDS?

Buddy-Building Strategies

CRABTREE
Publishing Company
www.crabtreebooks.com

Crabtree Publishing Company
www.crabtreebooks.com

Series Development, Writing, and Packaging:
John Burstein, Slim Goodbody Corp.

Editors:
Reagan Miller, Valerie Weber, and Mark Sachner,
   Water Buffalo Books

Proofreader:
Molly Aloian

Editorial director:
Kathy Middleton

Production coordinator:
Kenneth Wright

Prepress technicians:
Margaret Amy Salter, Kenneth Wright

Designer: Tammy West, Westgraphix LLC.

Photos: Chris Pinchback, Pinchback Photography

"Slim Goodbody" and Pinchback photos, copyright,
© Slim Goodbody

Photo credits:
iStock Photos: p. 5 (lower left), 17 (top)
Shutterstock: p. 4 (all), 5 (top, middle, lower right),
   13 (right), 14 (bottom), 16 (top), 17 (bottom),
   21 (top), 23 (bottom))
© Slim Goodbody: p. 1, 6, 7 (all), 8 (all), 9 (all), 10
   (all), 11 (all), 12, 13 (left), 14 (top), 15, 16 (bottom),
   17 (middle), 18, 19 (all), 20, 21 (bottom), 22, 23
   (top), 24, 25, 26, 27 (all), 28, 29

Acknowledgements:
The author would like to thank the following
children for all their help in this project: Stephanie
Bartlett , Sarah Booth, Christine Burstein, Lucas
Burstein, Olivia Davis, Eleni Fernald, Kylie Fong,
Tristan Fong, Colby Hill, Carrie Laurita, Ginny
Laurita, Henry Laurita, Louis Laurita, Nathan
Levig, Havana Lyman, Renaissance Lyman,
Andrew McBride, Lulu McClure, Yanmei
McElhaney, Amanda Mirabile, Esme Power, Emily
Pratt, Andrew Smith, Dylan Smith, Mary Wells

"Slim Goodbody" and "Slim Goodbody's Life
Skills 101" are registered trademarks of the Slim
Goodbody Corp.

Library and Archives Canada Cataloguing in Publication

Burstein, John
   Can we be friends? : buddy-building strategies / John Burstein.

Slim Goodbody's life skills 101)
Includes index.
ISBN 978-0-7787-4793-2 (bound).--ISBN 978-0-7787-4809-0 (pbk.)

   1. Friendship--Juvenile literature. I. Title.
II. Title: Buddy-building strategies.
III. Series: Burstein, John. Slim Goodbody's life skills 101

BF723.F68B87 2010   j158.2'5   C2009-903570-7

Library of Congress Cataloging-in-Publication Data

Burstein, John.
   Can we be friends? buddy-building strategies / John Burstein.
      p. cm. -- (Slim Goodbody's life skills 101)
   Includes index.
   ISBN 978-0-7787-4809-0 (pbk. : alk. paper) -- ISBN 978-0-7787-4793-2 (reinforced
library binding : alk. paper)
   1. Friendship in children--Juvenile literature. 2. Friendship--Juvenile literature.
Title. II. Series.

   BF723.F68G66 2009
   158.2'5--dc22

                                             2009022852

Crabtree Publishing Company

www.crabtreebooks.com   1-800-387-7650
Copyright © **2010 CRABTREE PUBLISHING COMPANY**. All rights reserved. No part of this publication may be reproduced, stored in a retrieval
system or be transmitted in any form or by any means, electronic, mechanical, photocopying, recording, or otherwise, without the prior written permission
of Crabtree Publishing Company.

Published in Canada
Crabtree Publishing
616 Welland Ave.
St. Catharines, Ontario
L2M 5V6

Published in the United States
Crabtree Publishing
PMB16A
350 Fifth Ave., Suite 3308
New York, NY 10118

Published in the United Kingdom
Crabtree Publishing
White Cross Mills
High Town, Lancaster
LA1 4XS

Published in Austra
Crabtree Publishin
386 Mt. Alexander Rd.
Ascot Vale (Melbourne
VIC 3032

CONTENTS

Words in **bold** are defined
in the glossary on page 30.

MAKING FRIENDS

Carla was feeling nervous. She was going to camp tomorrow, and she didn't know anyone there. Her best friend, Becky, was supposed to go with her. At the last minute, however, Becky's parents decided to go on a family vacation instead. Her parents told her not to worry. "You'll make lots of friends, dear." But Carla was not so sure.

On her first day at camp, Carla looked around at a sea of new faces. She was worried. What was she going to do now?

The First Step

If you want to make a new friend, you need to be brave. You have to walk over to somebody and start a conversation. If you wait around and hope someone will walk over to you, you may be waiting a long time.

Every time you talk to someone, you have a chance to make a friend. You can find good people who share your interests all around you. The more people you talk to, the better chance you have of making more friends. You won't become buddies with everyone you talk to, but keep trying.

I'm Slim Goodbody.

I know that everyone wants to have friends. Friends are people who care about you and look out for you. Friends are fun to hang out with and people you can talk to about anything that is on your mind. Friends, however, don't fall out of the sky or just show up at your door one morning.

I wrote this book to help you learn how to build strong, lasting friendships. You can do it. I can help!

Here are just a few of the places you might meet a new friend:

- In class
- In a club at school
- On the playground
- On the school bus
- In your neighborhood
- At the mall
- At a party
- On a sports team
- In the lunch line in the cafeteria
- At **church**, **mosque**, or **temple**

MAKING THE FIRST MOVE

Check out the kids around you. Figure out whom you might like to talk to first. See who looks interesting or nice. There might be a special look in her eyes, or you may like the way he smiles. You may have heard her telling jokes or seen a picture he drew in art class. You might even see someone who looks lonely and could use a friend. Whatever the reason, if something about that person catches your eye, you might be looking at a future friend.

Flash a Smile

It is just about time to go over and say hello. If the person you want to meet is looking at you, flash them a friendly smile. A smile sends a message. It says, "Hi, I'm a friendly person." The person might react in different ways:

• If the person smiles back, it means that he or she might be happy to meet you.

• Sometimes people are too shy to smile back. No smile may not mean that they don't want to talk with you. They may be just a little scared but would be happy if you walked over.

• If the person turns away, however, it probably means that now is not a good time to go over.

Go Over

Go over to the person. Smile and look her right in the eye. Now you're ready to start talking.

CONVERSATION CATCH

Having a conversation is a lot like playing a game of catch. Instead of throwing a ball to someone, you "throw" a sentence or two. Then your partner in the game "throws" a sentence or two back.

If you learn to "throw" the right kinds of sentences, the game is easier to play. For example, if your first "throw" includes a question, your partner has an easy "throw" back. He or she just has to toss you a simple answer.
Here is an example of how Conversation Catch is played. Try "throwing" the following:

"Hello. My name is _____. What's yours?"

Your partner "catches" the question. He tosses back his answer, "Ricky."

You catch his answer and throw back,

"Hi Ricky. I just moved to town. "What's fun to do around here?"

Your partner tosses back something like,

"We have a skate park."

Catch This

If you know the person's name, you can begin Conversation Catch with something you have in common. For example, try throwing the following,

"Do you know when our science project is due?"

Your partner tosses back,

"Next week."

You throw,

"What are you doing for your science project?"

Your partner tosses back, "A potato clock."

Now you have a conversation going.

Lend a Hand

If you see somebody who needs help, you can easily begin a game of Conversation Catch. For example, try throwing the following:

"Those boxes look heavy. Can I help you carry them?"

Your partner tosses back: "Sure. Thanks."

You throw, "Where are we taking these?"

He tosses, "Mr. Walker wants these boxes stored in the science room."

HOT TOPICS

Another kind of "throw" that works well is a simple statement about the weather.

For example, you toss out,
    "It sure is hot today."
Your partner throws back,
    "It sure is! I'm sweating."
You follow up with,
    "I was just about to get a drink of water. Do you want to come?"
Your partner tosses back,
    "You bet! Race you to the fountain!"

The next thing you know, you may be having fun with a possible new friend!

Ways to Praise

Another way to play Conversation Catch is to start by "throwing" an honest **compliment**. Think about how great you feel when someone says something nice about you. Doesn't it make you want to keep talking to that person? Here is an example of how compliments can work:

You toss out,
    "Your sneakers really look cool."
Your partner throws back,
    "Thanks."
You follow up with,
    "Do they help you run fast?"
Your partner says,
    "They sure do. Want to see?"

Once again, your Conversation Catch is working, and you can keep going.

Join In

If someone comes over and starts playing Conversation Catch with you, join in the game right away. Catch what he or she has said, and toss something right back.

Don't Give Up

Sometimes your Conversation Catch just won't work. Perhaps

- the other person is too shy, too busy, or not feeling well.

- he or she has enough friends already and doesn't want to give you a chance.

- he or she is just plain rude —and would you really want to be friends with someone with poor manners?

Don't get **discouraged**. Keep trying new people. Sooner or later, you will meet someone who might become a good friend.

CONVERSATION COLLECTION

You'll be a lot more comfortable playing Conversation Catch if you're prepared with topics to talk about. Pay attention to what is going on in school, in the news, in your neighborhood, and in sports. Think about what you really love to do that others might be interested in. Write down your list of conversation topics to help remember them. Avoid gossiping or talking meanly about other people. Instead, you could share:

- Something funny you heard in school
- An amazing science fact you read in the paper
- A trick your pet can do
- A sports event you saw on television
- An interesting book you read
- A holiday or vacation coming up
- A game you like to play

What Do You Like?

While you're talking, someone may ask your **opinion** about something. It may be about a show on TV, a basketball team, or your favorite food. Spend time thinking about the things you like to do and the people you admire. If someone asks you a question, you will then have an honest answer. This helps keep Conversation Catch going strong. Here are some examples of things to figure out:

- What kind of movies do you like?
- What do you like to read?
- What's your favorite hobby?
- Who is your favorite singer?
- Who is your favorite athlete?
  - What's your favorite subject in school?
  - Who is your favorite movie star?
  - What's your favorite sports team?
- What are your favorite games?

Topics We Share

Remember, no matter whom you are talking to, you always have something in common. Everybody has a family. Everyone is learning something in school. If you aren't sure what to say in a conversation, just talk about one of these subjects. Avoid gossiping or spreading rumors.

MISMATCH

Let's say you're well prepared and have a good conversation. After talking awhile, you might not feel the person would make a good friend. For example, he might seem too **immature** or seem unkind. She might seem too bossy or act like a know-it-all. You may discover the person is nice but doesn't like the same things you do.

Making friends is much easier with someone who shares some of your interests. For example, if you love chess, you'll probably want a friend who wants to play with you. If you love books, you'll probably want a friend who enjoys reading, too. You don't have to like the exact same things, but if you have very different interests it may be harder to become friends.

Trust Yourself

Whatever your reason for thinking or feeling that a friendship will not work, trust yourself. Friendship takes a lot of time and energy. You should feel excited about trying to build the friendship.

Sooner or later, you will find a good match. Once you do, go for it. But make sure you don't ignore old friends while you are making new ones.

Planting a Seed

Friendships don't happen overnight. They take time to develop and grow. Developing a friendship is a little like growing a flower. You need to be **patient**. You can't force a friendship or a flower to **blossom**. If you pour too much water on a flower seed, you will drown it before it has a chance to grow. You can also drown the seed of friendship by pouring too much attention on your new friend. Don't call all the time or stop by his or her house without being invited. If you allow a flower or a friendship to grow at its own speed, one day it will blossom beautifully.

IT TAKES TWO

You can't create a friendship all by yourself. You and your friend must work together to create a strong friendship. When you first plant the friendship seed, you both must do three important things:

- Be brave
- Spend time together
- Invite each other to your home

Be Brave

When people really want something to work out, they often get a little scared. They are afraid of being hurt or disappointed. To make a friend, you must be willing to take a risk. Your friend also has to take a chance. You need to tell yourself that even if the friendship does not work out, it's still worth trying.

Spend Time Together

Plan on meeting in the lunchroom or on the playground. Time together will give you a chance to get to know each other better. Share information about yourselves. Tell each other what you like and don't like to do. Learning about things you both like gives you more to talk about.

Invite Each Other Home

Of course, you have to first get permission from your parents. Think about what you will do when your friend arrives. Plan some fun indoor or outdoor activities. If you know your friend's favorite game, get the board ready. If she likes to play catch, make sure you have a ball around.

Plan activities you can do together. If you play a computer game, your friend might be left with nothing to do but watch. That will not be fun, and she might think you are being selfish.

Blossoming

The more time you spend doing things together, the more interests you will be able to share. You will grow in understanding. Understanding helps the seed of friendship blossom.

A GOOD BALANCE?

After spending time together, you may discover that you don't really want to be friends. Perhaps you don't have enough shared interests. You might realize your friend is not really that good a person. He or she might want you to take dangerous risks. He might be selfish and not want you to be friends with anyone else. She may always demand that you do what she wants to do. Or you might discover that the two of you get along really well. Then you need to work on keeping your friendship in balance.

yes
no

Seesaw

A healthy friendship is like a seesaw. Sometimes one person gets his way, and sometimes the other person gets her way. Sometimes you play at your friend's home. Other times you play at yours. Friends need to share **responsibility** for what they do and when.

If one person stays on the high end of the seesaw too long, the other person might just get off. Then the friendship comes crashing down.

Keep It Real!

You might feel your friend is not doing his share as a friend. If that's true, be honest and say so. Honesty is as important for growing a friendship as water is for growing a flower. You can't do without it.

If you're upset, tell your friend how you feel. If you bottle up your feelings, your anger will grow instead of your friendship. When you tell the truth, you can figure out a way together to make the friendship more equal.

Be honest about your good feelings, too. Let your friend know how much you enjoy his or her company. Finally, if you think your friend is heading for trouble, talk about it. Tell him why you think he may be making a poor choice.

KEEP YOUR PROMISES

Friends must be able to trust each other. An important way to build trust is to keep your promises. For example, if you tell a friend that you will call her, make sure that you do. If you don't, she may worry or feel you don't care. Think how you would feel if she promised to do something for you and didn't do it. Breaking your promise can harm a friendship, especially when it comes to secrets.

Keeping Secrets

If you share a secret with a friend, it means that you trust him enough not to tell anyone else in the world! If your friend shares a secret with you, he expects the same of you. **Betraying** a secret will often wreck a friendship.

Secrets can be big or small

- What you're writing about in English class
- What present you hope to get on your birthday
- Problems you are having at home
- Something you are worried or scared about

You may be worried about some secret your friend tells you. For example, a bully might be picking on your friend. In that case, try to convince your friend to speak to a trusted adult. The only time it is OK to reveal a friend's secret is if it means you can stop someone from getting **physically** hurt.

Jealousy

If you start feeling jealous of a friend, deal with the problem right away. Ask yourself, "What's more important, feeling good about my friend or feeling bad about him because he has something I want?"

You will probably realize that your friend is more important than any **possession**. Once this is clear, your jealous feelings should start to fade.

YOUR BFF

After you've spent a lot of time with someone, you may decide to become best friends. A best friend, or BFF (best friend forever), knows, understands, and cares about you more than any other friend in the world. You feel the same way about him or her. You may have other good friends, but none is as close. Best friends share their most private thoughts, feelings, and dreams. They trust and protect each other.

No one knows for sure what changes a regular friend into a best friend. When it happens, though, you know it.

Keep Watering

Never take a best friend **for granted**. Just because the flower of friendship has blossomed, doesn't mean you can stop watering it. You must still spend time together. You must both continue to share your thoughts and feelings. You must still find ways to be kind, helpful, and loving to each other.

One Way

Sometimes it happens that only one person in a friendship wants to be best friends. Let's say a friend of yours asks you to be best friends. But you are best friends with someone else. If that happens:

1. Be honest. Tell the person the truth.

2. Be kind. Tell the person you don't want to hurt his or her feelings.

3. Stay friendly. Tell the person you still want to be friends and hope he or she does, too.

It often happens that people only stay best friends for a while. For some reason, they both decide they like other people more. If this change happens, they can usually still stay friendly.

ONE WAY

SAVING A FRIENDSHIP

If you betray a trust or hurt a friend's feelings, you will probably fight about it. Either or both of you might say something hurtful. Your friend might tell you that your friendship is over.

If you want to save the friendship, sometimes an apology will work. Don't apologize, however, unless you really mean it.

You'll probably have only one chance, so think carefully about what you want to say.

Write your apology down, and practice it before you meet. Apologize face to face, not on the phone or in an email.

A Planned Apology

Here are some tips to help you figure out what to say:

1. Begin your apology by clearly stating what you said or did that was wrong.

2. Explain that you know how much your words or actions hurt your friend.

3. Do not offer reasons or excuses. An apology with an excuse is not a true apology.

4. Take full responsibility. Even if you feel your friend was partly to blame, this is your apology. It's not a chance to get her to apologize to you!

5. Tell your friend you have learned from your mistake.

6. Explain how important your friend is to you. Let her know how much she means in your life.

7. Ask if she will forgive you and give you a second chance.

8. If your friend accepts your apology, say, "Thank you."

9. If your apology is not accepted, say "Thank you for listening. If you ever change your mind, please let me know."

Sometimes one apology will lead to another. Your friend might apologize back. Don't count on it, however. If your friend does apologize, forgive her.

COMING TO AN END

Even when there is no fighting involved, deep and strong friendships sometimes come to an end. This can happen for many reasons:

- You stop being interested in the same things
- You get busy in school and sports and don't have enough time together
- You switch schools or move away to a new town
- You get a little tired of spending time together
- You meet a new friend you want to spend time with

Pulling Together

In some cases, you can try to keep the friendship going. If you or your friend have moved away or changed schools, you can phone and email each other. If one of you finds a new hobby, can the other learn to like the same thing?

Sad Endings

No matter how hard you try, sometimes you just can't stay friends. When friendships end, there are usually feelings of sadness and loss. A good friend has become part of you and your world. When the friendship ends, you lose a little bit of yourself. There may always be a warm place in your heart for your friend, but you'll probably feel a kind of emptiness as well. Endings are difficult for everyone. You might need to cry for a while. You might need to talk about your feelings with your parents or other friends.

After some time passes, you'll start to feel better. You'll remember the good times you had and you'll smile.

A GOLDEN RULE

Each day, try to do something to make a new friend or to keep your current friendships strong. Always be true to yourself, however. Never do something you feel is wrong just to make or keep a friend. Here's a kind of golden rule about friendships—

If you want to **HAVE** a friend you need to **BE** a friend

List things you can do each day to be a good friend. Your list might include:

- I will do something nice today for a friend.
- I will call a friend on the phone.
- I'll make a card for my friend's birthday.
- I will tell my friend why I like him or her.
- I will always try to help my friend reach his or her goals.
- I will let my friend know that he or she can talk to me.

A Very Special Friend

Before ending my book, I want to talk a little about the very best friend you can ever have. It is you, yourself. Many kids do not **appreciate** just how special they are. Please do not make this mistake. There is no one in the whole world exactly like you. There never has been and there never will be. You are one of a kind. That makes you very **valuable**.

This does not mean you cannot improve. You can learn to treat yourself with more respect. Here are some things you can do.

- Take care of your body. Eat well, exercise, and stay safe.

- Improve your mind. Read, study, imagine, and ask questions.

- Share your feelings.

- Develop your skills.

- Visit new places and make new friends.

As you become a better friend to yourself, you will become a better friend to others. When you appreciate and love yourself, you will have more to give and more to share.

Now You Know

Everyone can make friends if they try. Now that you know the steps to take, you can start building your friendships and watching them blossom.

GLOSSARY

appreciate To understand the value of something

betraying Telling someone something that is supposed to be kept secret

blossom To develop and grow in a healthful way

church A Christian place of worship

compliment A positive statement about someone

convince To cause someone to believe something

discouraged Having lost hope in something

for granted As a given; without thinking or appreciating. Taking someone for granted means not appreciating that person's special qualities or importance

immature Describes someone who acts younger than his or her real age

mosque A Muslim place of worship

opinion A person's belief in or thoughts about something

patient Able to wait for something to happen without becoming nervous or losing hope

physically Having to do with the body

possession Something that someone owns

praise Positive words about someone or something

responsibility Taking charge of what needs to be done

temple A Jewish place of worship

valuable Worth a great deal

BOOKS

Making Choices And Making Friends: The Social Competencies Assets. Pamela Espeland (Author), Elizabeth Verdick (Author). Free Spirit Publishing.

Friends: Making Them & Keeping Them. Patti Kelley Criswell (Author), Stacy Peterson (Illustrator). American Girl Publishing, Inc.

Making Friends (Thoughts and Feelings). Sarah Levete. Stargazer Books.

Every Kid's Guide to Making Friends. Joy Wilt Berry. W Pub Group.

How Kids Make Friends: Secrets for Making Lots of Friends, No Matter How Shy You Are. Lonny Michelle. Freedom Publishing Company.

WEB SITES

PBS Kids · ZOOM Home
pbskids.org/zoom/activities/do/friendshipbracelet.html
On this wonderful Web site, you can learn how to make a friendship bracelet.

Squigly's Playhouse
www.squiglysplayhouse.com/Postcards/Friendship.html
This fun site will allow you to email friendship notes to your friends. Be sure to get a parent's permission to log on.

Child and Youth Health
www.cyh.com/HealthTopics/HealthTopicDetailsKids.aspx?
p=335&np=286&id=1705#1
This Web site from Australia features a lot of information and fun activities about building friendships.

Kids' Space Connection
www.ks-connection.org
This is a safe and friendly site where children and school teachers can find pen pals from around the world!

Slim Goodbody
www.slimgoodbody.com
Discover loads of fun and free downloads for kids, teachers, and parents.

INDEX

About the Author
John Burstein (also known as Slim Goodbody) has been entertaining and educating children for over thirty years. His programs have been broadcast on CBS, PBS, Nickelodeon, USA, and Discovery. He has won numerous awards including the Parent's Choice Award and the President's Council's Fitness Leader Award. Currently, Mr. Burstein tours the country with his multimedia live show "Bodyology." For more information, please visit **slimgoodbody.com**.

Printed in the U.S.A.— C